POSITIVITY IS A MOVEMENT
Lyrics of Peace, Positivity and Encouragement
BY DELANO S. SMITH

WITHDRAWN

PREFACE

As a young boy growing up in The Bahamas, I thoroughly enjoyed writing short stories and lyrics. Whenever I composed any type of literature, I first thought about how my work would affect the reader. I imagined them becoming elated and self-confident at the conclusion of any of my compositions. When I decided to embark on the journey of writing this book, it truly began as one poem. A poem that created room and opportunity for others to be formed, nurtured, and eventually revealed to the world as a positive collection of lyrics.

My creations have been influenced by personal heroes such as Sir Lynden Oscar Pindling, Bob Marley, Mahatma Gandhi, Maya Angelou, and Martin Luther King, Jr. It is through their essence, historical events and present experiences that my literature exists. Being able to express my thoughts to the world is an honor and privilege, and I constantly embrace the opportunity to discuss positivity, encouragement, love, and other real life issues. Like a bird with no wings, I once did not have the ability to fly; however, once encouraged and exposed to positivity, I knew that I had no choice but to succeed. I decided to use my life lessons to encourage others on a daily basis, with high hopes that they would translate and relay the message of positivity.

First and foremost, I would like to thank God for making this all possible. I would also like to thank my family for all of the support that they consistently and meaningfully render. My father, Rudolph, my mother, Martha, my wife, my daughters, my mother-in-law, brothers, and last but not least, my grandmother, Merline. To all of you, I extend a heartfelt and spectacular 'thank you'. To my readers, I would like to thank you for taking the time to read my book, and I hope that you are positively influenced.

APPRECIATION OF LIFE

Breathing in the earth's oxygen
While processing my vivid thoughts
So much inner turmoil
Just need to find that inner peace

My writing of words on this paper
Serves as a temporary escape
But why do I, Why do we..
Try to escape our earthly challenges?

Every new day should be appreciated
Every new day should be approached with zest
All the struggles that come will not succeed
Because we can be beings of tactful precision

Every time you enjoy a meal
Think of it as your last
Savor every flavor of it
No exaggeration, just a state of mind

Every time you kiss your significant other
Think of it as your last kiss
Taste each other's lips
Let the passion ride, like a boat riding the waves

Every time someone offends you
Don't be tempted to act irrationally, forgive them
Teach them by how you respond
Do not judge them, show them

Always appreciate life as a great gift
And you will be appreciated now and when you depart
Remembered as an advocate of good living
So Appreciate Life, Appreciate Life, Appreciate Life

Delano Smith

BAHAMAS

Coconut palm trees, feel the beautiful calm breeze
Kneeling before God, with the beach at my knees
Democratic society, we can vote as we please
Good food, I really like my rice with some peas
Love my cracked conch, and of course my conch salad
Really missing my souse – I'm just being candid
Truly missing my *momma's* delicious Johnny bread
That breakfast morning stew, especially the fish head
No Imitation crab, I prefer real Crab and Rice
Guava Duff, what I wouldn't do to have a slice
Regattas at Homecomings keep the tourists coming
Our waters so clear, it really keeps me wondering
I remember playing and enjoying dominoes with *paps*
Start the game with winner pose, or double six perhaps
In The Bahamas, there are so many ways to relax
Some attend fish fries and others like the tracks
Tourist in my own country, some islands still unexplored
The Bahamas has so much talent, no longer ignored
I'm floored, but soon I think I'll need to take a flight
Back to The Bahamas, possibly this very night

BOMBS AT MARATHONS

Please explain it, this is very mind-numbing
Time is running out, and the bombs are still coming
Boston Marathon - celebrating the art of running
Negative schemes began, and dreams started crumbling
Innocent lives on the line, like a worm is bait
Hatred is the sinker, but we must uphold faith
WE as in mankind, WE, as in please find..
A quick remedy to this situation, please rewind
Senseless minds placing innocent lives in binds
Yielding frustrations of a very different kind
Some want to kill, but others just want to find..
A quick remedy to this situation, please rewind
Wherever you exist on this earth, you face corruption
We must try hard to limit our negative consumption
As hate consumes, and confuses us into having less trust
The wicked ones love that, please don't enhance their lust

Delano Smith

CHEATER'S PARADISE

Pepper words you speak with
Words you speak in secret
Not your husband speaking
Who is that you creep with?
Thought you had a spouse
Who is that inside your house?
Thought that you were married
Enjoyed being carried..
Over the threshold
Who is that your flesh holds?
Closely, closely, without a fear
Toasty, toasty, too hot in here
A penny for your thoughts
A dollar for your conscience
You finally got caught
Husband fed up with the nonsense

Long haired exotic girl
Nothing like your wife's curls
Thought you had a spouse
Why so quiet like a mouse?
Except when you're out of town
Spending money by the thou-
-sand, looks precious on the beach
Saying your *side* girl looks like a peach
Your wife planning special trips
You're chillin' with your special chick
Wife couldn't digest the thought of this
Now she's vomiting with her stomach sick
A penny for your thoughts
A dollar for your conscience
You finally got caught
Wife fed up with the nonsense

Positivity Is A Movement

Delano Smith

CRIME WAVES

Let Us
Have this moment of silence..
Acknowledging violent acts that have occurred
The unnecessary events in New Town Connecticut
Life so delicate, where is the human etiquette?
I represent a fraction, searching for peace
Religious harvest arrives, yet only few feast
We walk on two feet, but we're four feet from the end
Life is too short, but many desperately pretend
Faced with guns, corrupted by violence
Too many innocent lives are now resting silent

Let Us
Pray for the ones we love..
Looking above, and asking for guidance
From Killings in Nassau, to crimes across seas
Crime waves occur, even splashing on Belize
I can't believe that adults are shooting babies
Did that Earthquake increase the crime rate in Haiti?
Lately, too many violent acts occur
No Christopher Wallace, no Tupac Shakur
Less lyrical passion due to their early passing
Crime creates fear, but love is everlasting

DAUGHTERS (Dedicated to My Daughters)

Good daughters - their presence so positive
They beautify my life - I must acknowledge this
From the second they were born - life prominent
From the second they were born - love dominant
Love dominates while the devil's hate hibernates
Under my watch, I will keep their hearts safe
Under my watch, they're developing traits
Positive traits that will affect the human race

As they both look into my eyes, I see hope
Unique individualities, with the ability to cope
To deal with the trials and earthly tribulations
I hope they exhibit class in every situation
My vow to God, to love you both till the death of me
I pray to God, to keep you both stable mentally
No parental faction - your mom and I both love you
We receive great satisfaction, doing right by you

If anyone tried, or potentially dared
To hurt, to harm you, well they better be prepared
I abstain from violence, but for you I will get physical
I would risk my existence, even though I'm not mythical
Never understood the love my parents felt for me
Until that October 19th, when I held Sade
My first-born baby, emotions overtook me
I was a newfound man - the reality check shook me

As the days go by and you both grow older
Into mature women, the world will seem colder
The unexpected pressures, universal depressions
Cherish all experiences, and take away the lessons
However, never let a soul take your beliefs
And never, let them break your mental physique
Together, protect and love each other through it all
And Forever, Daddy will never let you fall

DEVIL NOT GOOD

The thought process of when God created man
He gave us so much wisdom, but it is hard to understand..
The way we treat each other, casting morals asunder
So many love the flash, but lack supporting thunder
Maintain all that is good, in this flesh that God provides
If the devil infiltrates, that can lead to mental homicide
He will only lead you as far as you let him
MISLEAD you, with such potent and seductive venom

Then like vapors, our dreams start to escape us
Then ultimately, we become recyclable, like papers
Ultimately, the term 'friend' transforms to 'associate'
If the power returns, associates want to negotiate
Look in your in rearview, let your past help you decide
Reject that PEER view, some friends are not on your side
Sometimes due to jealously, hidden on the inside
However, keep your hearts pure and the devil won't reside

Delano Smith

DEVOUR LIFE

With the right seasonings
I devour this life with justified reasoning
Tell me, is there something you believe in?
If you have no goals, then why are you breathing?
So deceiving, misconceptions left me thinking
Perceived life differently - that's why I 'm speaking
To educate the youth, give the youth the truth
There's a chance to succeed, a chance to relieve
The stress that exists, and forms angry fists
Resist fear, I encourage you to persist
And whenever tempted, you must appear relentless
Visions too good, possibly I could have dreamt this
But I meant this...form of encouragement
Adequately give your brain substantial nourishment
Without knowledge, your mind is hungry for days
Increasing your chances of being easily swayed
The devil is persuasive, and jealously invasive
But all the negativity will never replace this..
Positive energy the Lord has willingly provided
So I devoured life, when strength and will collided

Positivity Is A Movement

Delano Smith

DREAM WOMAN

Your skin, perfectly soft with a splendid tone
Your scent, the culmination of fragrances in your perfume
Beautiful or gorgeous, whichever adjective you choose
Is the description of the one I hope not to lose
Your touch is enough to make a whole city quiver
Sensations as to which no earthquake could even deliver
It gives birth to visions, to be more exact, fantasies
Which consists of love, adventure, and trips across seas

Your smile, is the epitome of clarity and truth
It embodies the qualities of pureness and youth
To look at you, is like looking at the sun
Staring too long, tends to leave one stunned
Therefore, I absorb your beauty in glances
With you, I hope to not to need any second chances
Every first with you shall be memorable and good
Our eyes speak to each other, never misunderstood

Your heart is generous, appreciative, and sweet
It even thanks its blood for making it beat
This stems into your everyday actions
Putting others first, creating instant satisfaction
You are the essence of a modern day Mother Theresa
If you could, you would give memories to those with amnesia
There really is no limit to your consistent kindness
This is felt by the poor, and even those who have blindness

Delano Smith

ENVIRONMENT

Corruption seduces, environments tend to influence
You MUST rise above it, or watch the skies plummet
Blind to some facts, you must insightfully react
Positively influence those with whom you make contact
These streets are a college, drugs the professor
Fiends listen so hard they're addicted to the lectures
Many negative environments, surely there is an escape
So think outside the box, and use different shapes
Use your mind's mass to lose the negative weight
Use your brain power, empower yourself for hours
Discover new ways of making the devil cower
Displaying new traits that the haters can't negate

Positivity Is A Movement

Delano Smith

HUSTLER'S ANTHEM

I'm hungry and malnourished
So I eat from the Hustler's plate
Such food has me Hustling in my dreams
My brain is stronger in this state

I wake up in a deep sweat
My brain appears to be doing overtime
The world doesn't pay me time and a half
Have to work even harder to get what is mine

The Hustler's blood, is universally tied
No discrimination, against any color
It's all about that thick motivation
And the rewards it will help us discover

Remember, the haters will come
But your dreams will make them quickly go
It is up to that Hustling mentality
To make your inner worth grow

When my thoughts smell funky
I rinse with that Hustler's Scope
So when my tongue starts persuading
My ideas come out fresh and dope

A Hustler's weapon is the brain
So we must blast them with our thoughts
A Hustler's energy is very addictive
No worldly drugs needed to support

I pledge to fight today's battles
To use that Hustling power from within
To build my family's bright future
Before any discouragement sets in

So let all the naysayers rejoice
Let them waste their mental juices
Show them better, and love them
Then give them the peace sign, deuces

I LOVE MY ENEMIES

Those who discourage, don't have the necessary courage
Utilize their discouragement, and rise high above it
I love it - fortified rhymes for these hideous times
Keep your brain alert, and keep reading between the lines
Neglect the haters and wave 'em off – BYE HATER
Eagerly awaiting your next move – HI WAITER
Let the haters live in denial while you live in the sky
Make your dreams come true, stop living in your mind
Economy's horrendous, but possibilities endless
Believe in your future, your perception will defend it
Be strong and resourceful, never easily hurt
If you don't have a beach, create pools in deserts
Many get offended, because you hustle and strive
Never let them diminish your potent energy drive
This is what you worked for, sweat, bled, hurt for
If they want to take it away, then that – means - war

This is for my foes – I will never let you compromise
Because I know my position, where my loyalties reside
Every time I see a hater, it makes me feel so able
So I enable myself, and use my PASSION as a cradle
We must let our personalities exude great confidence
When haters try to attack, laugh it off, be nonchalant
Some perceive it as arrogance - they know not what you faced
Where were they when obstacles were in your face?
We must thank God for life lessons, they're indirect blessings
Pressuring us to fly above all the worldly indiscretions
So when the evil ones bring the hate, you do not participate
Just use it as inspiration, reload and concentrate
See I monitor their kind, and then make 'em mentally bleed
They're trying to figure me out, I'm just trying to succeed
I'm not an enigma, just constantly misunderstood..
But I show love to my enemies, so in the end, It's all Good!

Positivity Is A Movement

Delano Smith

I REMEMBER

I do remember, The World Trade Centers
Why couldn't the terrorists trade peaceful letters
Words of peace and harmony released
Love invoked - no human beings deceased
Such a tragedy - the blatant inhumanity
I remember seeing the smoke - watching some choke
Choke up with tears, this threat was too near
Of Middle Eastern descent? Then you felt the stares

I remember, vividly sitting in class
Professor on the phone, repeating the word 'crash'
The city's been attacked - school closed for the day
Terrorists the predator - twin towers the prey
Parents thinking that I'm in the city for an interview
My frat brother thinking his dad is in harm's view
Very sad time, there were just so many tears
Is this a movie? Will the end credits appear?

I remember, seeing victims being punished on both sides
Innocent American bodies falling from the sky
Good Muslims being tortured for the actions of few
The few extremist Muslims that made fear come true
They instilled fear, in the heart of a nation
This became clear, in every single conversation
The fear breathed hatred - the hatred made patriots
Even the silent types started to make statements

I remember, volunteering at ground zero
Surrounded by the spirits of the true heroes
It's unfortunate, but tragedy created unity
Should it have come this? Such a twisted bliss
Hopefully, we all learn peace and remain united
And Hopefully, this peace is eternally invited
I remember, seeing vigils everywhere
But most of all, I remember the fear

JUNE 10TH

Blood pressure building in my ice cold veins
It seems, like it's very hard to maintain
I remember that night very clearly it seems
I remember revenge was clearly calling my name
In your city, heard somebody got shot
Was it 4 times, or maybe it was five...
I was just hoping that my brother was still alive
I was just hoping that my brother would survive
Your own wife didn't even know where to find you
That's when I pictured those bullets right behind you
Called every hospital searching for the truth
The next thing I know I'm on Highway 82
My wife right beside me, squeezing my hand
I think on that night, I became her biggest fan
For supporting me, through each and every hour
No physical tears, but I cried mental showers
Wanting to devour all enemies in sight
Found you at hospital late that night
Police officer escorted me to your room
He was taking precaution, preventing your doom
Preventing your demise, I transformed into a spy
False friend showed up, got his access denied
Looked at me in wonderment, and then asked, "Why?"
Then he quickly left, he saw the anger in my eyes
I had no fear, I really didn't care
I was just extremely baffled, this night wasn't clear
I almost gave in, adhered to the devil
Should I get a gun? My thoughts disheveled
Didn't know how it happened, so who could I trust
I just trusted in God, which seemed like a must
Went downstairs so that I could find a minister
To administer a prayer for all that was sinister
Brother had no motion as minister held devotion
Prayer so powerful out came my emotions
Physical tears, it then became clear
God would save your life, and answer our prayers

Positivity Is A Movement

Delano Smith

KEEP THE LYRICS COMING

...the mental incarceration
Releasing my thoughts, my mind off probation
Talking to myself, one on one conversation
Conversation leaked, to each and every nation
State of the world resting heavy on my mind
How can I sit back and watch it steadily decline?
...readily define the hatred that exists
Black on black crime, can't blame the racists
No more patience, people even killing babies
Where's the moral code, no respect for the ladies
Every other song, has profanity in it
Every other movie seen has a sex scene in it
World moving too fast, devil corroded the limits
Slow down just a little, please recognize the gimmicks
Wives killing husbands- husbands killing wives
While the other family members remain traumatized

For the Trayvon Martins, all across the world
The battered shattered women, who are no longer girls
The people in the street, with no food to eat
The sexually abused, and the falsely accused...
One day, someday, maybe cometh peace
One day, someday, the Lord will come in peace
He will talk to us - alive or deceased
Better stay prepared - be an advocate of peace
What happened to Martin Luther's Kingdom of dreams?
What happened to not worshipping material things?
Some governments corrupt, who can we trust?
In God I trust - until I see the dust
Oh boy, oh man - how times have changed
I see more negativity, and fewer good things
I embrace the goodness, I hope to magnify
If I influence one -hopefully it multiplies

Delano Smith

LIFE IS GRAND

Now I understand - life is so grand
Standing ovation - given to God's plan
From the trees to the birds and the bees
From the cars and houses, to hidden luxuries

Now I understand - life is so fine
Filled with music - all God's design
Wind blowing the trees - making them dance
Mother Nature really leaves us in a trance

Now I understand - why we help each other
On some level, we're all sisters and brothers
Common goal in mind - we can coexist
Common vision at heart - we can defeat the mist

Now I understand - life is so grand
Thousands of memories captured by vast lands
Remember; never take life's beauty for granted
Another world awaits, it will leave you enchanted

Positivity Is A Movement

LYRICAL ENIGMA

Concepts so strong, they suffocate the lyrics
How else to deliver, except in subtle specifics
Subconsciously some hate, yet consciously I embrace
Meditate on that hate while putting dinner on plate
Their zombie ambitions lower their inhibitions
Negative discussions are their favorite traditions
Their favorite position is that of the pessimist
Relentlessly, I fight them with a peasant fist
Trust me, the devil lurks around many corners
Inflicting pain, the devil's looking for mourners
It's so appalling, call the pall bearers...
The devil killing spirits - end is coming near us

Best option - stay positively inspired
By those examples who prematurely expired
Like Bob Marley, such a calm, dynamic spirit
Many play his music, but they don't really hear it
It's apparent in our actions how they create factions
So surreal how pain can give persons satisfaction
Be the change that you want to see in the world
Ghandi was right, I wish that for my little girls
They arrived in a world that is filled with temptations
Temptations tempt nations, translation segregation
We are not perfect, but we can all live as one
Because ONE DAY, the true ONE will come...

MERLINE HANNA

Many years have passed, since I've last seen you
You were the only grandparent that I really knew
I miss your smile, and the jokes that you gave us
All the mischief we did, yet you forgave us
Addressed you as *Ma'am*, more frequently *Grammy*
Classy, and fully invested in your family
Your favorite grandson was Winslow, we knew that
Had a special bond with him, I really hope he knew that
Life so puzzling, filled with so much uncertainty
Mother gave me the news - stomach started hurting me
Couldn't believe you were gone - tears in my eyes
In retrospect, that's when destructive behavior arrived
Sometimes, I regret moving so far away from home
Spent many years away from you, and hope to see you soon
Merline Hanna, you were such a dedicated grandmamma
I remember you watching the Days of Our Lives drama
Wish I had the chance to recite this poem to you
But all I have are memories, looking in Life's rearview
However, I will never forget the lessons you taught us
Especially, that there's always someone you can trust
And all our memories I will pass onto my little girls
Through good and bad times, you were always a great Pearl
You left the world with thoughts that keep giving
If your spirit is here, I'd like to thank you for living

MIND DOLLARS

Intellectual escapades transformed me into a renegade
Thinking too much for so long, over two decades
The cards that I've played, were the only cards dealt
Every time I write a lyric it has to be heartfelt
I've been through it all - from mind rags to fake riches
Mind riches have arrived, and I anticipate the snitches
In addition, I'm ready for the ones who wear hate as clothing
Positively vicious; my schemes got your brains exploding
Consistently do the best that I can, with the least that I have
Give me a quarter cent, this dude will turn into a half
Unguided beginnings can lead to illustrious endings
This is not about cash, but rather, what your mind is spending
Intellectual dollars gained from the knowledge attained
My brain is just a fortress that is keeping me so sane
You inane haters breed such infinite possibilities
So I will live in the stars, this is a hustler's astronomy

Delano Smith

MS. POETRY

So beautiful - even when she cries
Her tears caress the flowers, as they scent the sky
Skies ascend the lies, on another plane she resides
Mind, body, and spirit soulfully intertwined
Such a graceful nexus, so I don't need a Lexus
Your mind possesses enough luxury to perplex us..
All..never fail never fall, that's your motto
Beauty one in a billion - billionaire lotto
Lucky to know you - more grateful to show you
How you have impacted those that always explore you
Readily adore you, and the calmness you represent
So beautiful - Ms. Poetry is heaven-sent

NEW IMAGINATION

Imagine life, without hidden agendas
Sweeter than Splenda, every day with our sender
Maker, creator, God, the inevitable source
Positive being, providing us with adequate force
Force to imagine, believe, and ultimately succeed
Steady doing deeds, based on not so foreign creeds
Bible essential, need to read it more often
The intention is seeking hard hearts to soften
The intention is to someday really comprehend
Just want to be in the right when facing the end
Meanwhile, I enjoy life in a peaceful fashion
Spreading love and joy, no need for the clashing
Smiles of my daughters give me hope all the time
I reciprocate...never hesitate, because I relate

Delano Smith

NO GLOSS

Hypercritical, my own toughest critic
Mind always on the move, I'm mentally Kinetic
Mentally projecting my rise from these ashes
Never failing LIFE's test, I took the right classes
Had the wrong lens, but I had the right glasses...FRAME
Corrected vision enables me to MAINTAIN
For those that know me, that metaphor goes very DEEP
Until I see I peace, I guess I will cease to sleep

Like I said before, I will rise from these ashes
Mashing the gas in impeccable fashion
I take risks like a stuntman, but never do stunts
Few have my back, but I know MANY that FRONT
If you feel my pain, you can sense my desires
While some that inflict pain are treated like Messiahs
This Backwards world filled with many hidden talents
Yet there are many hearts that are filled with malice

I've never liked hatred, it's making me complacent
Placed in dilemmas where I'm constantly faced with....
Faced with those sheep that only love the basics
With ground level dreams, they will never see spaceships
I'm never cocky, I'm only promoting confidence
Sophisticatedly promoting, subtle nonchalance
And if you know me, I'm trying to stay positive
Real Lyrics – I promise, no gloss in this

Stick to your dreams, because the devil is relentless
Consuming your soul, giving you a death sentence
Ruining your goals, a part of the Death Census
Many shaking their heads, saying it was all senseless
Use your 6th sense, stop using the 5 common
Erupt your thinking, stop leaving your brain dormant
New thinking occurs – live in the Post Modern
Spread positive thinking, let your voice be storm winds

Delano Smith

OVERRATED

Racism is overrated
All these crimes are overrated
Wife-beating is overrated
You don't agree? Then you are overrated

I keep it poppin' like a can of tasty Pringles
Never play my lady, never play cassette singles
I have respect, so neglect will never follow
I try not to fight, so I abstain from shooting hollows

Nowadays, violence is getting really sick
From Guerrilla Warfare, to the Bloods and Crypts
We really need to get our lives on track
Back to Martin Luther King, Bring the Good Back

I wonder how he'd feel, knowing that we kill
Kill each other all day, and then we lay still
Six feet under, Six feet deep!
Soul escaping your body, physical presence is weak!

No good to the world, you're in eternal sleep
Your children left behind, now they eternally weep
Too many people in the world are acting like sheep
All they do is follow, their minds are too hollow

We need to up the ante, read some good literature
Maybe read something about Toussaint Louverture
Intellectual Excitement, let me stimulate your ear
If your feet are too tired, all you need is your mind's chair

Don't be afraid, let your mind take a stance
This learning thing is dope, such a chemical romance
If you're not ready, it means you're afraid to mature
Let us learn from our past, we must never ignore

To all the cowards, you classified chumps
You remind of the materials we place in the dump

OVERRATED – CONT'D

You – Are – Gar-bage!
Please tell me, how do you manage?

To put horrible marks on a pretty lady's face
She's in so much pain, yet you feel no disgrace
If I see it happening, I will put you in your place
You have such poor class, and she, the incorrect taste

But I leave it up to God, no need to increase the violence
Every day I close my room door, and utter to him in silence
God, please forgive me for using any profanity
I just had to let it out, to avoid the insanity

I've got chips on my shoulders, but don't we all
Got looked at the wrong way, while shopping in the mall
Store owner was white, and I guess I was Mr. Black
He coldly stared at me, as I went from rack to rack

Man, if I was weak I think I would've been crying
I didn't shed a tear, but on the inside, I was dying
After so many years, racism can still be so thick
We need a heavenly demolition crew to give it a kick

Finally, I won't apologize for being ever so blatant
I'm tired of folks making, and abiding by stupid statements
Mainly the ones we presume to have intelligence
You know the ones, they never assume negligence

PERFECTION

As I touch your body, I respect it as God's temple
Something only a higher being could've possibly assembled
Beautiful hair, beautiful skin, an overall beautiful you
As long as I'm around you, I enjoy a magnificent view

Girl, I have a mental picture of you stapled to my brain
When I miss you, I visit and admire your perfect frame
So even if I'm asleep, blindfolded, or turn blind
There's nothing or no one, that can erase you from my mind

Your body's on the beach being warmed by the sand
The ocean is kissing your toes, I should be an envious man
The sun starts glistening, I guess it's plottin' on you too
My eagerness and confidence is obstructing its view

I'm really not jealous, I'm just a bit overzealous
My love integrity is the greatest, different from the other fellas
I'm overflowing with confidence, and you're radiating such joy
Together we're explosive, there's no need to be coy

I am a seeker of perfection, you are the holder of that trait
I am a seeker of perfection, how long will you make me wait
I am a seeker of perfection, you are embedded in my mind
I am a seeker of perfection, our love will begin in due time

There are no duplicates, no fakes, no close carbon copies
Can't be digitalized, or transferred to 3.5 disk floppies
I get a glance of your perfection, from the top of the world
Supported by God's invisible hands, I'm searching for you girl

I appear to be floating, but love is just making me high
There's no need for marijuana, your love is how I get by
I'm not spittin' any game, filling your head with propaganda
Our time on earth is too short, let me be your only romancer

Your energy is atop a mountain, that I'm beginning to climb
My boots kick down unnecessary dirt, that is to be left behind

PERFECTION – CONT'D

Boots representing my soul, dirt representing any bad qualities
When I meet you at the top, there will be no place for anomalies

I kiss your lips with my fingers, next, I kiss them with my lips
Your mind is like wine, I enjoy taking mature sips
Our mental frames matched, before our physical beings even met
Beautiful lady, you are perfect, and this moment I will never forget

I am a seeker of perfection, you are the holder of that trait
I am a seeker of perfection, how long will you make me wait
I am a seeker of perfection, you are embedded in my mind
I am a seeker of perfection, our love will begin in due time

REPERCUSSIONS

Hear the percussions when the repercussions hit
What goes around comes around - not a myth
Your actions cause reactions, and have consequences
When the wise ones speak, you need to be the apprentice
Come to your senses, and see through moral lenses
Open up your heart, and put down your defenses
Defenseless tactics used in the act of gaining knowledge
Attracted to the dirty, with hopes of giving them polish
Yet I am dirty too, we all are dirty - not just few
We all commit SINS, some look for repentance
Others look for assistance in the form of drugs
To fuel their fantasies, then sweep them under the rug
But God is always watching, and God always cautions
He knows when we commit all of our moral abortions
Forgetting all of the morality that he instilled in us
Repercussions will follow, unless in God we trust
Some folks brainstorm with intentions of Brainwashing
Oh God! This mental laundry is truly exhausting
And THEY, don't even try to do it in proportion
Be careful, because THEY, move quickly without caution

Positivity Is A Movement

Delano Smith

ROOTS OF POSITIVITY

People often ask, why are you so positive?
I often say, that's the only way to live
The only way to give back, to truly impact
Fortify the world, keep the goodness in tact
Even on my worst day, I promote positivity first
Never hurt the world, we should increase its worth
I've observed and I've learned, how to keep this balance
From Gandhi to Martin, keeping peace is a challenge

Naysayers testing me, saying I want to deceive them
Trust me, there's a good reason I believe in..
Maintaining the love, and quickly spreading the peace
Let my spirit try hard, even after I am deceased
Were they there when my brother got shot, left bleeding?
Or when that car wreckage occurred on another evening?
Were they there, when the gun was at my head in New York?
No they weren't, but they still want to blindly talk

So please forgive me, if I smile through all seasons
Trust me, I've got so many different reasons
If I do lose my temper, I try quickly to regain...
My sense of calmness, from anger I will abstain
Blood pressure rising, heart attack on the horizon
Stressful situations may lead to your demise in...
This world, beautiful world so appealing
So it doesn't make sense to embrace negative feelings

Positivity Is A Movement

Delano Smith

RUN

Your life broken - choose to fix it
Wise words spoken - choose to listen
Recognition and repair are necessary
To be negligent of fault is not hereditary
Because YOU choose your eventual path
God gives formulas, and you calculate the math
No flaws in the formulas, yet we make excuses
No laws apply, yielding destructive uses
Destructive uses of tools that were meant for good
Then YOU yield thoughts of being misunderstood
In my ear aloud, blasphemy rings!
Run back to your morals, before catastrophe sings

SCENT OF HEAVEN

A piece of me is constantly searching for peace
A part of me is partially set to release
Release this positive beast that internally resides
Prey on negativity, make the devil run and hide
I preside over my mind like a president over lives
I pray for the negativity - may we all survive
Survive the tyranny, hunger, the insatiable greed
Some wish to see me fail, my only wish is to succeed

My desires are inspired by a fire that is higher
I admire Jesus' sacrifice, therefore I inquire
Therefore, I go to church to prove the devil is a liar
I admire Jesus' sacrifice, therefore I aspire
Aspirations of a man searching for His Highness
Reminders in the form of miracles always remind us
Sublimeness, how else can I truly define this?
If ye can give in sight, why not ye give in blindness?

Erase the jealousy, and bring forth the empathy
Put yourself someone's shoes, walk that empty street
And never be discrete about your past indiscretions
If experience taught you, then you should pass the lesson
Past transgressions led to future confessions
Erase the malfeasance, witness the newfound blessings
I'm suggesting change with the necessary means
I guess I'm suggesting change with God as our King

As I refine my thoughts like a fine wine import
I decline the devil's invitation, he's trying to extort
Abuse my assets in an attempt to create frailties
Misuse my 6th sense, in an attempt to frame me
Couldn't frame me, because I'm not a perfect picture
Full of sin, but now I'm being filled with Scriptures
No more affliction, God is my new addiction
A scent of heaven expressed, in this vivid depiction

Positivity Is A Movement

Delano Smith

SHE TOLD ME, I TOLD HER

She told me, there's not much to believe in
When your own kind is doing the most deceiving
That her kind is even doing the physical beating
Mistreating her - sometimes left her bleeding
And racism played a role, he's black she's white
Her parents didn't really share much in her delight
High as a kite, she said at times she loved the sky
Escaping her nightmares, making fantasies multiply
Why me, Oh God? Is the question she asked?
She did so much good, yet she still finished last
Vividly grasped, the concept of achieving her goals
But felt too discouraged and decided to fold

I told her, your parents are wrong - are you kidding me?
All your dreams are filled with so much validity
Attending college - actively enhancing your knowledge
That FREE abuse they gave, now they need to PAY homage
You're modernly enslaved, you need to break those shackles
Date who you want to date, even when they can't relate
As long as the guy is respectful and goal-oriented
Then build a good union, and proudly present it
There's no need to get high, that might lead to addiction
Don't escape what you can overcome, keep your convictions
My prediction is that you will be very successful
Start enjoying life and watch it become less stressful

SKIN COLOR AND PEACE

Little kids being ridiculed just because of race
Racists use the term 'nigger', but not in my face
I really wonder - why does skin color even matter?
I truly ponder why so many focus on the latter
Colorblind to skin is what I will forever be
Some see color, I only see personalities
Others see stereotypes, but we all bleed red
Less stereotypes will lead to less bloodshed

Confederate flags waving, yet I ride through those streets
Smiling and being positive to all those I meet
When it comes to spreading peace, I am never discrete
Spreading peace every day, my work is never complete
Never delete the thought and idea, of being a peace soldier
Serious warfare, we need strong and deliberate chauffeurs
To carry this Peace Initiative boldly on their shoulders
Even a small dose of peace can win someone over

As I'm writing these lyrics, many will hate them
But These Truths exist, not even Houdini can escape them
I deliver hopeful suggestions, soulful recommendations
Hopefully leading to emotions and feelings of elation
Black, White, Hispanic, Indian, Asian
WHO CARES! Just be of good moral persuasion
Especially if you have children, you must teach them well
The hatred of skin color really needs to be dispelled

Positivity Is A Movement

Delano Smith

SUN CAN'T BURN ME

Sun can't burn me, unless God lets it
Hatred can't touch me, God too impressive
Forgave transgressions, taught me many lessons
God left the impression – I'm surrounded by blessings

Sun can't burn me, morality is my sunblock
Inject morality in prisons, leave them cell shocked
We all deserve a chance, some never take it
Some love the clothes, yet their hearts are naked

Sun can't burn me, my brain is the shade
Knowledge is my power – intellectual renegade
I encourage kids to read, but some look at me funny
Funny how some countries end up being ruled by dummies

Sun can't burn me, I'm a different breed
 One must first believe, for God to help them succeed
We are all unique, yet we try to be the same
Don't care about my critics, spreading peace is my game

Sun can't burn me, I'm too deep in the struggle
Too deep in this mindset, peace will end this struggle
Threaten me with violence, I'll never be afraid
Because God will silence all negativity made

Sun can't burn me – the moon gave me confidence
Promises in struggles sometimes lead to prominence
We must remain rich in heart, to enrich our spirits
Richly read your bibles, there is much to inherit

Sun can't burn me – I feel so ALIVE
We can do ANYTHING, keep a focused mind
Resign all thoughts of negativity and jealousy
Focus on your dreams, strive for them relentlessly

Sun can't burn me – Courage too strong
God's mercy is stronger, helps me to last longer

SUN CAN'T BURN ME – CONT'D

So much turmoil, it heats the world like coils
Then emerge the vultures, looking for the spoils

Sun can't burn me, because you're still reading this
If my words affect one, then there is hope in this
Spread the peace and love, be a Peace Chauffeur
Drive this potent energy, be a Peace Soldier

Positivity Is A Movement

THE EFFECTS OF JAZZ

Midnight assassin, clashing with vivid nightmares
The emergence of good music erases all fears
I'm influenced by the styling of jazz music
Such a love conduit, heavily loving these acoustics
Loving the Coltrane, such a stimulant to the brain
Whatever your mood, music helps you to maintain
Maintain your sanity, a basic sense of humanity
So mentally lifted, the disappearance of gravity
Very terrific pleasure, not simplistic to measure
Gratifying, implying, and trying to uncover hidden treasures
Treasures of the mind, now poverty has declined
Now richer in spirit, constantly enriching mankind

THE JEREMIAH POEM

Jeremiah prophesied about Jerusalem's destruction
We face different equations, but use the same functions
Same outcomes, as if we never learn from our past
Some yearn for the past, to correct mistakes that last
I'm giving you hidden messages so that you may unfold
Not that difficult, I reiterate what has been told
Extremely bold with this passion of mine, these lyrics
I hope to edify, spread love, and have one holy critic

That holy critic is only one that can wholly judge
Fully understand my character, never hold a grudge
I thank God for giving us such great wisdom
For giving us the chance to ensure his will is done
Act on that chance, we don't know when he'll return
Spread his word and love, make sure others learn
Willingly discern what is right from wrong
Willingly come to terms, and always remain strong

Jeremiah, Jeremiah, may you prophesy again please
Apparently we need reminders to constantly remind us
Sunshine exists here, but many have on their blinders
Pretending that evil doesn't constantly lurk beside us
Jeremiah, Jeremiah, may you please encourage..
And forever may your message linger, never discourage..
God's children, and those that truly hope to become..
Apart of the goodness, a part of God's Kingdom

Positivity Is A Movement

Delano Smith

THE LOVE

Green light - your love ready to go
Green life – some have jealousy on tow
But you know to succeed, you must be unstoppable
Very surgical - every challenge is operable
Magician with your mind, a regular Copperfield
Every chance you get, you try to get a feel..
Of love's aura - you hope to explore the..
Depths of its existence - hear your persistence
Always witnessing beauty personified
Seeing newness every day, the love is so alive
Striving, outlasting, forever surviving
If the love gets hurt – it will buy slings
Supporting the love will further nourish it
Flourish it to the point where loyalty fits..
Now the love, is pure like a dove
Now souls are intertwined - that's the love

THE PICK-UP PUT-DOWN

Put down the guns - pick up your conscience
Pick up a book - rise above this nonsense
Put down the jealousy - pick up the love
Put down the hate – I think I see the doves
Critical times lead to hyperactive minds
We tend to forget, leaving all good behind
We control our own minds, mental monopoly
Stress-free, is what we should truly strive to be

Put down the fake talk - pick up the truth
Put down the bad examples - pick up the youth
Pick up the role models - put down the crime
Pick up society, put down deceased lives
Critical times lead to hyperactive minds
We tend to forget, leaving all good behind
We control our own minds, mental monopoly
Stress-free, is what we should truly strive to be

Put down the nightmares - pick up the good dreams
Pick up the avid dreamers - the Martin Luther Kings
Put down the troublemakers - pick up the peacemakers
Pick up democracy - put down political shakers
Critical times lead to hyperactive minds
We tend to forget, leaving all good behind
We control our own minds, mental monopoly
Stress-free, is what we should truly strive to be

Pick up the families - put down the missing dads
Pick up the privacy - put down the lying tabs
Pick up our young women, put down the pregnancies
Pick up those strong women - they were meant to be
Critical times lead to hyperactive minds
We tend to forget, leaving all good behind
We control our own minds, mental monopoly
Stress-free, is what we should truly strive to be

Positivity Is A Movement

Delano Smith

TIRED YET INSPIRED

Please tell me - where is the peace?
I try to maintain but I need to release
Release this tension from a complicated mind
Walking in my mind like I'm walking in a mine...
Field, feels like I'm ready to explode
I'm becoming tired, and seek an inspirational mode
Men killing babies, gangs going crazy
Chances are Slim and most of us Shady

I'm tired of thugs trying to prove something
There's always a choice, no need for body counting
Shooting off rounds, sound the alarms
Police on the scene, dead bodies on the ground
How can we exist in a world like this?
Let us stop the killings, and create the bliss
Martin Luther King didn't dream of this
Stop the killings, and create the bliss

Fatherless children and deadbeat dads
The drugs on the streets travel like nomads
Deadbeat moms with no open arms
No love for the kids, so the kids bear arms
If you have sex, and produce those babies
Protect those babies, and raise those babies
Teach them the many different principles of life
Never give up on them, always give a fight

Oh God, My Lord, I'm getting tired
Many negative issues - I must stay inspired
Friends, let us talk about the friends
Many of you fake, can you relate friends?
Here is your knife, you can have it back
Back still healing from the unexpected attack
But that is alright, all I have is love for you
This world can change - we only need a new view

41

UNHEARD CRIES

The cries of a child being uttered in the far distance
Each cry seemingly represents a story that needs to be told
These cries get weaker as they become quickly displaced
Displaced by the loudness of a city that's in haste

Maybe it is easier for the city to be loud and ignore
Ignore the massive pain being felt by this youth
The child is left unheard, and eventually loses emotional feeling
Crime, drugs, and bonds with negativity all become appealing

Afterwards, we hear the media delivering news of new crimes
I blame our society for this cycle, which could have been avoided
Most of those drugs certainly did not have to be sold and used
All of those kids should not have been physically and mentally abused

If only society took the time to carefully listen
Some of the younger generation may have a better chance
Especially the ones growing up with no birth parents, wondering their worth
The ones who latch on to anything, subconsciously thinking they are dirt

On the other hand, maybe such social elements are actually needed
Maybe it is a test from God, to see how we cope with certain problems
Certain problems in society that will probably never go away
But if carefully analyzed will cost less human beings to pay

So the challenge here is to minimize all that is negative
Even though negativity is inevitably a part of the world's balance scheme
However, LISTEN carefully when a child is not speaking, but yet deeply crying
It may be the comfort of your voice, upon which he or she is relying

Positivity Is A Movement

Delano Smith

WHAT THESE WORDS MAY BRING...

Listen...to what these words may bring...
Sit down for a moment, and hear the birds sing
Hear the chirping...dissect their lifestyle
So conceited we are beings living in our own minds
Living our own trials, forgetting the trials of others
Daughters without fathers, sons back talking mothers
In your mind, they are just unnecessary others
In my mind, they are permanently sisters and brothers
Some brothers by the dozens bred my multiple fathers
Approached the mother, and she said it didn't matter
But it does when promiscuous actions lead to crime
Brothers of different fathers now all doing dimes
Prison sentence - repercussions are relentless
Let us prevent this, and properly utilize senses
Put down our defenses, and heed good advice
The ultimate goal should be to lead a good life

Delano Smith

<u>WIFE</u>

The concept of real love is lost in these modern times
I conceptualize, romanticize, and realize..
The truth to your being, is found in your heart's eyes
Using your to heart to see, so your vision never lies

But it lays the foundation for different situations
Frustrations capsized by heavier motivations
With you, I feel invincible doing all that it takes
With you, I know that I can make earthquakes shake

I guess former heartbreaks led us to this place
So fascinating, the tender beauty of your face
But the first beauty I found was in your inner grace
Even through our tough times that never gets misplaced

Sometimes we act in haste, and then we think late
That opposite order, leading to chaotic disorder
Order is restored, good role model for our daughters
You're gorgeous in many ways, love never monotonous

There is no other, I don't even think to ponder
Why ruin what is great, why put that greatness at stake
Many ladies try to tempt, but I never take the bait
No forbidden apples for me - that was Adam's mistake

Even though I hate our fights, I still do love them
It brings out our passion, love is everlasting
Love is enraging, poetically engaging
I'm poetically inclined to define your fine design

I will never resign from this post as your husband
I've seen some in love, but the others don't love them
No love returned, unrequited love discerned
So fortunate to have you, that lesson I learned

I cherish how you exhibit your exquisite personality
For some love is rare - for us its formality

WIFE – CONT'D

Now you got me caught up in this storm of love
Hurricane raging, amidst the storm was a dove

That's what I love about you, you always find peace
You revive my heart when I expect it the least
Fervent heartbeats, love never disappointing
We got baptized together, the Lord ever anointing

Lord bless our union, I pray for longevity
For all the naysayers, I pray that you're hearing me
I love this woman, I love my wife
I love how I love her, I love my wife

WIFE BEATER

Where to begin? There's so much to discuss
Much to my disgust, the cowards remain unjust
Ignorant men, nonchalantly beating women
Their time is coming, I constantly see omens
Sons learn the habits, and daughters remain abused
Such cowardly actions, God will not excuse
I recuse myself, because it might get personal
Hands on my daughters will yield hands not merciful

Mr. Wife Beater, I hope you hear me
I am your conscience, you should stay near me
Tough and strong? There's always someone stronger
You won't be beating on your wife for much longer
I hope these lyrics bring tears to your eyes
Internally tear you apart, you are despised
Dear Mr. Wife Beater, I hope you hear me
Dear Mr. Wife Beater, I hope you hear me

Well God bless the dead, some women die from this
By the hands of a man - I'm really getting pissed
Black eyes, dark shades, and the make-up hide..
The bruises, his lack of self-esteem just oozes
Ladies, seek help, embrace faith, and get strong
In this society, the wife beaters don't belong
Abusive men, seek help and get strong
Or suffer the wrath for recklessly doing wrong

Dear Mr. Wife Beater, I hope you hear me
I am your conscience, you should stay near me
Tough and strong? There's always someone stronger
You won't be beating on your wife for much longer
I hope these lyrics bring tears to your eyes
Internally tear you apart, you are despised
Dear Mr. Wife Beater, I hope you hear me
Dear Mr. Wife Beater, I hope you hear me

Positivity Is A Movement

Delano Smith

WORDS

Tell me, why so much error in this era?
Sippin' on the Visine won't help you see clearer
Lacking lyrical hygiene, they speak beyond measure
Same word they offend with, they use it for pleasure
My endeavor to be clever, specifically whenever
Pull the switch, adjective, be imaginative
Can I live in a world where words don't forgive?
Or maybe I'm wrong, and it's all relative

Intellectually celibate, let your wisdom escape
No longer imprisoned, your mind transcends hate
Creating new debates while voices develop bass
Lack of sense leads to words uttered with no taste
Such role models, with no goals to follow
Listen to ambitions of the kids that have sorrow
Don't show them to a world where words project fear
Subject them to a world where we're positively sincere

Positivity Is A Movement

Delano Smith

YOUR STRUGGLE

I could never think about giving up
That is not me, I wouldn't be living up...
To my expectations, I'll beat the tribulations
Negative situations lead to my haters elating
I won't participate in, their blatant disregard
Let them mock my dreams, I will fight from the heart
I will rock from the start - have a concrete finish
Supernatural ignition - my drive won't diminish

These lyrics are for you if you feel the struggle
The haters will talk, let your actions be the muzzle
Their puzzled, unable to put the pieces together
Remember, success should be your primary endeavor
No matter the weather, you ARE the hurricane
Storm after your dreams, with a passion in your veins
Especially, when it seems that it is all in vain
Just do it, you don't really have the time to explain

Fact is, the moment of truth has arrived
Struggling for success while you struggle to survive
Keep your legs on the ground, and mind in the sky
With astronaut visions your dreams won't subside
Work hard, work hard, the long run is coming
You will get what is owed, you shall be summoned
Summoned by the very sweet taste of success
You can feel it, they can see it, you have been blessed

ABOUT THE AUTHOR

Delano Smith was born in Nassau, Bahamas, and completed his high school career in The Bahamas. He graduated from St. John's University in Queens, New York, with a Bachelor of Science in Economics. He went on to further his education at Texas A&M in Commerce, Texas, where he received his Masters of Science in Business Management. Even though he has been business oriented for most of his career, his first love has always been writing.

Delano is the son of Rudolph and Martha Smith, and is married with two daughters. He has three siblings, and his hobbies include reading, playing basketball, learning, writing, and running. His mother Martha Hanna-Smith, is author of the popular Bahamian book, *Book Medicine in Bahamian Folk Tradition*.

Made in the USA
Charleston, SC
11 September 2013